This book belongs to

. . . .

. . . .

. . . .

. . . .

FAITH LISTS

FAITH LISTS

Your spiritual life in lists

Illustrated by
Olivia Holden

First published in Great Britain in 2019

Society for Promoting Christian Knowledge
36 Causton Street
London SW1P 4ST
www.spck.org.uk

British Library Cataloguing-in-Publication Data
A catalogue record for this book is available from the
British Library

ISBN 978–0–281–08204–9

Typeset by Viki Ottewill
First printed in India by Thomson Press
Subsequently digitally printed in Great Britain

Produced on paper from sustainable forests

Contents

List your favourite ways to connect with God

_____

_____

_____

_____

_____

_____

_____

_____

_____

_____

_____

_____

_____

_____

_____

_____

I want to Encourage you IN your FAITH, But I ALSO Want to BE ENCOURAGED by yours

Romans 1:12

List people who inspire you in your faith

_____

_____

_____

_____

_____

_____

_____

_____

_____

_____

_____

_____

_____

_____

_____

_____

List churches that you've attended

_____

_____

_____

_____

_____

_____

_____

_____

_____

_____

_____

_____

_____

_____

_____

_____

We ARE closer TO GOD WHEN we are ASKING questions THAN WHEN We think WE have THE answers

Rabbi Abraham Joshua Heschel

List questions that you'd like to ask God

_____

_____

_____

_____

_____

_____

_____

_____

_____

_____

_____

_____

_____

_____

_____

_____

_____

_____

Weeping MAY stay through THE Night BUT Rejoicing COMES in THE morning

Psalm 30.5

List Bible verses that bring you joy

List spiritual leaders you'd love to meet or wish you had met

_____

_____

_____

_____

_____

_____

_____

_____

_____

_____

_____

_____

_____

_____

_____

_____

_____

_____

Be thankful
in all
Circumstances

1 Thessalonians
5.18

List opportunities or possessions that you are thankful for in your life

_____

_____

_____

_____

_____

_____

_____

_____

_____

_____

_____

_____

_____

_____

_____

_____

_____

_____

List ways that you see God in the world around you

_____

_____

_____

_____

_____

_____

_____

_____

_____

_____

_____

_____

_____

_____

_____

_____

_____

Garden of Gethsemane

List spiritual places that you want to visit

_____

_____

_____

_____

_____

_____

_____

_____

_____

_____

_____

_____

_____

_____

_____

_____

_____

Wisdom IS
FAR more
Valuable
than RUBIES
NOTHING you
desire CAN
COMPARE
with it
Proverbs 8.11

List the best pieces of wisdom you've heard, read or learnt yourself

_____

_____

_____

_____

_____

_____

_____

_____

_____

_____

_____

_____

_____

_____

_____

_____

_____

List your favourite Christian authors

WAIT
for the
Lord
BE strong
and TAKE
HEART
and
FOR
THE Wait
Lord.

Psalm 27·14

List Bible verses that give you courage

List major moments in your faith life

LET YOUR
light shine
BEFORE others
THAT they may
see your GOOD DEEDS
and glorify YOUR
FATHER IN
Heaven

Matthew 5·16

List causes and charities that you'd love to support

_____

_____

_____

_____

_____

_____

_____

_____

_____

_____

_____

_____

_____

_____

_____

_____

List your favourite hymns or worship songs

_____

_____

_____

_____

_____

_____

_____

_____

_____

_____

_____

_____

_____

_____

_____

_____

List the qualities that you admire most in your church leaders

_____

_____

_____

_____

_____

_____

_____

_____

_____

_____

_____

_____

_____

_____

_____

_____

THE *Lord*
your GOD goes
With YOU;
he will NEVER
leave you
NOR FORSAKE
you

Deuteronomy 31·6

List Bible verses that bring you comfort

List your prayers for the future

Our HEARTS are restless UNTIL they find REST in God

St Augustine

List favourite Christian quotes that you've heard or read

silent Retreat

List spiritual activities or practices that you'd like to try

Be strong AND courageous DO NOT be AFRAID Do not BE DISCOURAGED for the Lord YOUR GOD will be with you WHEREVER you GO

Joshua 1.9

List times that you've stepped out in your faith

_____

_____

_____

_____

_____

_____

_____

_____

_____

_____

_____

_____

_____

_____

List people you'd love to meet in heaven

For God so loved the WORLD that HE gave his ONLY Son THAT whoever BELIEVES in him, should not PERISH but have eternal life

John 3:16

List your favourite Bible verses

_____

_____

_____

_____

_____

_____

_____

_____

_____

_____

_____

_____

_____

_____

_____

_____

List people you're praying will come to know God

_____

_____

_____

_____

_____

_____

_____

_____

_____

_____

_____

_____

_____

_____

_____

List some favourite things about your church

But the fruit of the Spirit is love, joy, PEACE, patience, kindness, GOODNESS, faithfulness, gentleness and self-control

Galatians 5:22-23

List characteristics that you'd like God to develop in you

_____

_____

_____

_____

_____

_____

_____

_____

_____

_____

_____

_____

_____

_____

_____

_____

List your favourite Christian bands or worship leaders

_____

_____

_____

_____

_____

_____

_____

_____

_____

_____

_____

_____

_____

_____

_____

_____

_____

Cast your cares on the Lord AND he WILL SUSTAIN you; he will NEVER let the RIGHTEOUS be shaken

Psalm 55.22

List Bible verses that help when you're worried

List your favourite Christian books

_____

_____

_____

_____

_____

_____

_____

_____

_____

_____

_____

_____

_____

_____

_____

_____

List the best sermons you've heard

I thank my God EVERY time that I REMEMBER you

Philippians 1:3

List people you are thankful for in your life

_____

_____

_____

_____

_____

_____

_____

_____

_____

_____

_____

_____

_____

_____

_____

always BE prepared to give an answer to EVERYONE who asks you to give the Reason FOR the HOPE that you have

1 Peter 3:15

List the reasons for your faith in God

List prayers that have been answered

I can
DO ALL THINGS
through
Christ who
STRENGTHENS
me

Philippians 4.13

List Bible verses that you'd like to commit to memory

_____

_____

_____

_____

_____

_____

_____

_____

_____

_____

_____

_____

_____

_____

_____

_____

List your favourite Christian radio shows or podcasts

List things that you feel God has said to you

List your favourite Bible characters and why

GOD is
OUR refuge
and
STRENGTH,
an ever-present
HELP in
trouble

Psalm 46.1

List situations that you'd like God to intervene in

This is my command: love each other

John 15·17

List ways in which you try to show God to those around you

_____

_____

_____

_____

_____

_____

_____

_____

_____

_____

_____

_____

_____

_____

_____

List seasonal traditions that help you to remember God

_____

_____
_____

_____

_____

_____

_____

_____
_____

_____

_____

_____

_____

_____

_____
_____

_____

_____

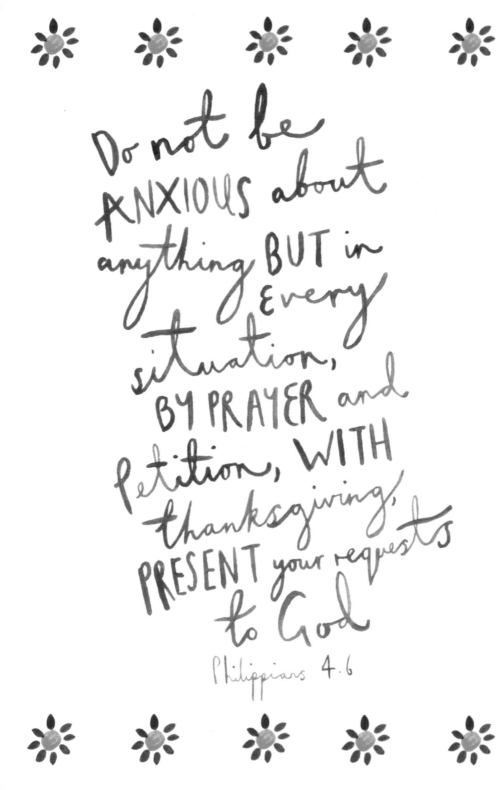

Do not be ANXIOUS about anything BUT in Every situation, BY PRAYER and Petition, WITH thanksgiving, PRESENT your requests to God

Philippians 4.6

List your prayers for friends and family

List what you'd like to be remembered for when you're gone

_____

_____
_____
_____
_____
_____
_____
_____
_____
_____
_____
_____
_____
_____
_____
_____

List your favourite spiritual places

For God has not
given us a
Spirit of fear
but of power
and of
Love and of
a Sound mind
2 Timothy 1·7

List the ways in which God might be asking you
to step out of your comfort zone

List your prayers for the world around you

_____

_____

_____

_____

_____

_____

_____

_____

_____

_____

_____

_____

_____

_____

_____

_____

List passions that you feel are God-given

_____

_____
_____
_____
_____
_____
_____
_____
_____
_____
_____
_____
_____
_____
_____
_____

FOR I am convinced that
NEITHER death nor life
neither ANGELS nor demons,
neither the present nor
the future,
NOR any POWERS, neither
HEIGHT nor depth,
nor anything else in all
creation, will be ABLE
TO SEPARATE us from the
LOVE of God
that is IN
CHRIST Jesus our Lord
Romans 8.38-39

List Bible verses that have personal significance for you

List inspirational Christian speakers

LOVE so Amazing, so Divine, Demands My Soul, my life, my ALL

Isaac Watts

List your favourite lyrics from hymns or worship songs

The Lord is my light and my SALVATION; Whom shall I fear? The Lord is THE STRENGTH of my LIFE; Of whom shall I be afraid?

Psalm 27.1

List Bible verses that encourage you

List the things that get in the way of you telling others about God

_____

_____

_____

_____

_____

_____

_____

_____

_____

_____

_____

_____

_____

_____

_____

_____

List the ways that you've felt encouraged in your faith

_____

_____

_____

_____

_____

_____

_____

_____

_____

_____

_____

_____

_____

_____

_____

_____

ASK and it will be GIVEN to you;

SEEK and you will FIND;

KNOCK and the DOOR will be Opened to you!

Matthew 7:7

List what you would ask God for if you could ask for anything

_____

_____

_____

_____

_____

_____

_____

_____

_____

_____

_____

_____

_____

_____

_____

_____

List your favourite Bible verses that praise God

_____

_____

_____

_____

_____

_____

_____

_____

_____

_____

_____

_____

_____

_____

_____

Jesus Christ Is the same yesterday, today AND forever

Hebrews 13:8

List which aspects of God's character you value the most

_____

_____

_____

_____

_____

_____

_____

_____

_____

_____

_____

_____

_____

_____

_____

_____

Notes